My State
PUERTO RICO

By Christina Earley

TABLE OF CONTENTS

Puerto Rico 3
Glossary 22
Index 24

A Crabtree Seedlings Book

Crabtree Publishing
crabtreebooks.com

School-to-Home Support for Caregivers and Teachers

This book helps children grow by letting them practice reading. Here are a few guiding questions to help the reader build his or her comprehension skills. Possible answers appear in red.

Before Reading:

- What do I know about Puerto Rico?
    - *I know that Puerto Rico is made up of islands.*
    - *I know that Puerto Rico has beaches.*
- What do I want to learn about Puerto Rico?
    - *I want to learn which famous people were born in Puerto Rico.*
    - *I want to learn what the official flag looks like.*

During Reading:

- What have I learned so far?
    - *I have learned that San Juan is the capital of Puerto Rico.*
    - *I have learned that El Yunque National Forest gets more than 100 billion gallons (379 billion liters) of rain a year.*
- I wonder why...
    - *I wonder why the national flower is the Flor de Maga's flower.*
    - *I wonder why the Cabo Rojo Wildlife Refuge has salt lakes that are pink.*

After Reading:

- What did I learn about Puerto Rico?
    - *I have learned that Mosquito Bay glows with blue light made by tiny animals.*
    - *I have learned that the national animal is the coqui.*
- Read the book again and look for the glossary words.
    - *I see the word **pyramid** on page 5, and the word **capital** on page 6. The other glossary words are found on pages 22 and 23.*

PUERTO RICO
¡Hola! My name is Angel. Welcome to Puerto Rico! It is a **territory** of the United States.

I live in Aguada. It is along the **shore** of the Atlantic Ocean.

The only **pyramid** in Puerto Rico is in my town.

Puerto Rico is a group of islands in the Caribbean Sea. The **capital** is San Juan.

Fun Fact: San Juan is the largest city in Puerto Rico.

The national animal is the **coqui**.

The Flor de Maga's flower is the national flower.

My family and I like to explore Old San Juan. Fortaleza Street has so many interesting things to see!

Fun Fact: San Juan was **founded** in 1521 by Spanish explorer Juan Ponce de León.

Puerto Rico's flag has red and white stripes. It also has a blue triangle with a white star.

Cabo Rojo Wildlife Refuge has salt lakes that are pink!

Fun Fact: The forest gets more than 100 billion gallons (379 billion liters) of rain a year.

I enjoy hiking at El Yunque National Forest. I like to see the waterfall at La Coca Falls.

It is fun to see fish when I go snorkeling off Flamenco Beach.

Mosquito Bay glows with blue light made by tiny animals.

Actress Roselyn Sánchez was born in Puerto Rico. MLB outfielder Roberto Clemente was also born in Puerto Rico.

Fun Fact: Sila María Calderón, the first woman to be governor of Puerto Rico, was born in San Juan, Puerto Rico.

The Guánica State Forest has exciting bike trails.

I like to visit Los Morrillos Lighthouse. The view of the Caribbean Sea is beautiful!

Glossary

capital (cap-ih-tuhl): The city or town where the government of a country, state, or province is located

coqui (koh-kee): A small tree frog that's yellow, green, or brown in color

founded (found-ed): Created or set up

pyramid (pir-uh-mid): A large structure with a square base and four triangular sides that come to a point at the top

shore (shor): The land along the edge of a body of water

territory (ter-ih-tohr-ee): An area of land that belongs to or is connected with a government or a particular country

Index

Aguada 4, 5
coqui 8
El Yunque National Forest 14, 15
Mosquito Bay 17
San Juan 6, 7, 10, 11, 19
Sánchez, Roselyn 18

About the Author

Christina Earley lives in sunny South Florida with her husband and son. She enjoys traveling around the United States and learning about different historical places. Her hobbies include hiking, yoga, and baking.

Written by: Christina Earley
Designed and Illustrated by: Bobbie Houser
Series Development: James Earley
Proofreader: Melissa Boyce
Educational Consultant: Marie Lemke M.Ed.

Photographs:
Alamy: IanDagnall Computing: p. 18 right; REUTERS: p. 19
Shutterstock: Dennis van de Water: cover; Terri Butler Photography: p. 3, 23; Wirestock Creators: p. 4, 17, 23; Ruben Santiago Martinez: p. 5, 23; Pyty: p. 6, 22; ESB Professional: p. 7; Falko Duesterhoeft: p. 8, 22; Mr. Arun: p. 9; Polina LVT: p. 10-11; Sean Pavone: p. 11, 22; railway fx: p. 12; NS Foto: p. 13; Dennis van de Water: p. 14; Cesar Zapata-Lozada: p. 14-15; Sahani Photography: p. 16; Kathy Hutchins: p. 18 left; stockphotofan1: p. 20; Photo Spirit: p. 21

Crabtree Publishing

crabtreebooks.com 800-387-7650

Printed in the U.S.A./072023/CG20230214

Published in Canada
Crabtree Publishing
616 Welland Avenue
St. Catharines, Ontario
L2M 5V6

Published in the United States
Crabtree Publishing
347 Fifth Avenue
Suite 1402-145
New York, New York, 10016

Library and Archives Canada Cataloguing in Publication
Available at Library and Archives Canada

Library of Congress Cataloging-in-Publication Data
Available at the Library of Congress

Hardcover: 978-1-0398-0532-3
Paperback: 978-1-0398-0564-4
Ebook (pdf): 978-1-0398-0628-3
Epub: 978-1-0398-0596-5